THE POEMS

OF

CHARLOTTE BRONTË

(CURRER BELL)

* – In 'Poems' by CB, EB & AB

CONTENTS.

POEMS OF CHARLOTTE BRONTË.

PILATE'S WIFE'S DREAM.

I'VE quench'd my lamp, I struck it in that start
  Which every limb convulsed, I heard it fall—
The crash blent with my sleep, I saw depart
  Its light, even as I woke, on yonder wall:
Over against my bed, there shone a gleam
Strange, faint, and mingling also with my dream.

It sank, and I am wrapt in utter gloom;
How far is night advanced, and when will day
Re-tinge the dusk and livid air with bloom,
And fill this void with warm, creative ray?
Would I could sleep again till, clear and red,
Morning shall on the mountain-tops be spread!

I'd call my women, but to break their sleep,
Because my own is broken, were unjust;
They've wrought all day, and well-earn'd slumbers steep
Their labours in forgetfulness, I trust:
Let me my feverish watch with patience bear,
Thankful that none with me its sufferings share.

Yet Oh, for light! One ray would tranquillize
My nerves, my pulses, more than effort can;
I'll draw my curtain, and consult the skies:
These trembling stars at dead of night look wan,
Wild, restless, strange, yet cannot be more drear
Than this my couch, shared by a nameless fear.

All black—one great cloud, drawn from east to west,
Conceals the heavens, but there are lights below;
Torches burn in Jerusalem, and cast
On yonder stony mount a lurid glow.
I see men station'd there, and gleaming spears;
A sound, too, from afar, invades my ears.

Dull, measured strokes of axe and hammer ring
From street to street, not loud, but through the night
Distinctly heard—and some strange spectral thing
Is now uprear'd—and, fix'd against the light
Of the pale lamps, defined upon that sky,
It stands up like a column, straight and high.

I see it all—I know the dusky sign—
A cross on Calvary, which Jews uprear
While Romans watch; and when the dawn shall shine
Pilate, to judge the victim, will appear—
Pass sentence—yield Him up to crucify;
And on that cross the spotless Christ must die.

Dreams, then, are true—for thus my vision ran ;
Surely some oracle has been with me,
The gods have chosen me to reveal their plan,
To warn an unjust judge of destiny :
I, slumbering, heard and saw ; awake I know,
Christ's coming death, and Pilate's life of woe.

I do not weep for Pilate—who could prove
Regret for him whose cold and crushing sway
No prayer can soften, no appeal can move ;
Who tramples hearts as others trample clay,
Yet with a faltering, an uncertain tread,
That might stir up reprisal in the dead.

Forced to sit by his side and see his deeds;
  Forced to behold that visage, hour by hour,
In whose gaunt lines the abhorrent gazer reads
  A triple lust of gold, and blood, and power;
A soul whom motives fierce, yet abject, urge—
Rome's servile slave, and Judah's tyrant scourge;

How can I love, or mourn, or pity him?
  I, who so long my fetter'd hands have wrung;
I, who for grief have wept my eyesight dim;
  Because, while life for me was bright and young,
He robb'd my youth—he quench'd my life's fair ray—
He crush'd my mind, and did my freedom slay.

And at this hour—although I be his
wife—
He has no more of tenderness from
me
Than any other wretch of guilty life ;
Less, for I know his household privacy—
I see him as he is—without a screen ;
And, by the gods, my soul abhors his
mien !

Has he not sought my presence, dyed
in blood—
Innocent, righteous blood, shed
shamelessly ?
And have I not his red salute withstood ?
Ay, when, as erst, he plunged all
Galilee
In dark bereavement — in affliction
sore,
Mingling their very offerings with their
gore.

Then came he—in his eyes a serpent-
smile,
Upon his lips some false, endearing
word,
And through the streets of Salem clang'd
the while
His slaughtering, hacking, sacrilegious
sword—
And I, to see a man cause men such
woe,
Trembled with ire—I did not fear to
show.

And now the envious Jewish priests have
brought
Jesus—whom they in mock'ry call
their king—
To have, by this grim power, their ven-
geance wrought;
By this mean reptile, innocence to
sting.
Oh! could I but the purposed doom
avert,
And shield the blameless head from
cruel hurt!

Accessible is Pilate's heart to fear,
 Omens will shake his soul, like autumn leaf;
Could he this night's appalling vision hear,
 This just man's bonds were loosed, his life were safe,
Unless that bitter priesthood should prevail,
And make even terror to their malice quail.

Yet if I tell the dream—but let me pause.
 What dream? Erewhile the characters were clear,
Graved on my brain—at once some unknown cause
 Has dimm'd and razed the thoughts, which now appear,
Like a vague remnant of some by-past scene;—
Not what will be, but what, long since, has been.

I suffer'd many things—I heard foretold
 A dreadful doom for Pilate,—lingering woes,
In far barbarian climes, where mountains cold
 Built up a solitude of trackless snows:
There he and grisly wolves prowl'd side by side,
There he lived famish'd—there, methought, he died;

But not of hunger, nor by malady;
 I saw the snow around him, stain'd with gore;
I said I had no tears for such as he,
 And lo! my cheek is wet—mine eyes run o'er,
I weep for mortal suffering, mortal guilt,
I weep the impious deed, the blood self-spilt.

Weeps not because she loves him but because she has compassion & humanity

More I recall not, yet the vision spread
  Into a world remote, an age to come—
And still the illumined name of Jesus shed
  A light, a clearness, through the unfolding gloom—
And still I saw that sign, which now I see,
That cross on yonder brow of Calvary.

What is this Hebrew Christ?—to me unknown
  His lineage—doctrine—mission; yet how clear
Is god-like goodness in his actions shown,
  How straight and stainless is his life's career!
The ray of Deity that rests on him,
In my eyes makes Olympian glory dim.

The world advances; Greek or Roman rite
  Suffices not the inquiring mind to stay;
The searching soul demands a purer light
  To guide it on its upward, onward way;
Ashamed of sculptured gods, Religion turns
To where the unseen Jehovah's altar burns.

Our faith is rotten, all our rights defiled,
  Our temples sullied, and, methinks, this man,
With his new ordinance, so wise and mild,
  Is come, even as He says, the chaff to fan
And sever from the wheat; but will his faith
Survive the terrors of to-morrow's death?

* * * * *

I feel a firmer trust—a higher hope
Rise in my soul—it dawns with dawning day;
Lo! on the Temple's roof—on Moriah's slope
Appears at length that clear and crimson ray
Which I so wished for when shut in by night;
Oh, opening skies, I hail, I bless your light!

Part, clouds and shadows! Glorious Sun appear!
Part, mental gloom! Come insight from on high!
Dusk dawn in heaven still strives with daylight clear,
The longing soul doth still uncertain sigh.
Oh! to behold the truth—that sun divine,
How doth my bosom pant, my spirit pine!

This day, Time travails with a mighty
birth;
This day, Truth stoops from heaven
and visits earth;
Ere night descends I shall more surely
know
What guide to follow, in what path to
go;
I wait in hope—I wait in solemn fear,
The oracle of God—the sole—true God
—to hear.

MEMENTOS.

ARRANGING long-locked drawers and
shelves
Of cabinets shut up for years,
What a strange task we've set ourselves!
How still the lonely room appears!
How strange this mass of ancient treas-
ures,
Mementos of past pains and pleasures;
These volumes, clasped with costly
stone,
With print all faded, gilding gone;

These fans of leaves, from Indian trees—
These crimson shells, from Indian
seas—
These tiny portraits, set in rings—
Once, doubtless, deemed such precious
things;

Keepsakes bestowed by Love on Faith,
And worn till the receiver's death,
Now stored with cameos, china, shells,
In this old closet's dusty cells.

I scarcely think, for ten long years,
A hand has touched these relics old;
And, coating each, slow-formed, appears
The growth of green and antique mould.

All in this house is mossing over;
All is unused, and dim, and damp;
Nor light, nor warmth the rooms discover—
Bereft for years of fire and lamp.

The sun, sometimes, in summer enters
The casements, with reviving ray;
But the long rains of many winters
Moulder the very walls away.

And outside all is ivy, clinging
To chimney, lattice, gable grey;
Scarcely one little red rose springing
Through the green moss can force its
way.

Unscared, the daw and starling nestle
Where the tall turret rises high,
And winds alone come near to rustle
The thick leaves where their cradles
lie.

I sometimes think, when late at even
I climb the stair reluctantly,
Some shape that should be well in
heaven,
Or ill elsewhere, will pass by me.

I fear to see the very faces,
Familiar thirty years ago,
Even in the old accustomed places
Which look so cold and gloomy now.

I've come, to close the window, hither,
  At twilight, when the sun was down,
And Fear my very soul would wither,
  Lest something should be dimly shown,

Too much the buried form resembling,
  Of her who once was mistress here ;
Lest doubtful shade, or moonbeam trembling,
  Might take her aspect, once so dear.

Hers was this chamber ; in her time
  It seemed to me a pleasant room,
For then no cloud of grief or crime
  Had cursed it with a settled gloom ;

I had not seen death's image laid
In shroud and sheet, on yonder bed.
  Before she married, she was blest—
Blest in her youth, blest in her worth ;
  Her mind was calm, its sunny rest
Shone in her eyes more clear than mirth.

And when attired in rich array,
  Light, lustrous hair about her brow,
She yonder sat, a kind of day
  Lit up what seems so gloomy now.
These grim oak walls even then were
      grim;
  That old carved chair was then an-
      tique;
But what around looked dusk and dim
  Served as a foil to her fresh cheek;
Her neck and arms, of hue so fair,
  Eyes of unclouded, smiling light;
Her soft, and curled, and floating hair,
  Gems and attire, as rainbow bright.

Reclined in yonder deep recess,
  Ofttimes she would, at evening, lie
Watching the sun; she seemed to bless
  With happy glance the glorious
      sky.
She loved such scenes, and as she gazed,
  Her face evinced her spirit's mood;
Beauty or grandeur ever raised
  In her a deep-felt gratitude.

But of all lovely things, she loved
  A cloudless moon on summer night;
Full oft have I impatience proved
  To see how long her still delight
Would find a theme in reverie,
  Out on the lawn, or where the trees
Let in the lustre fitfully,
As their boughs parted momently
  To the soft, languid summer breeze.
Alas! that she should e'er have flung
  Those pure though lonely joys away:
Deceived by false and guileful tongue,
She gave her hand, then suffered wrong;
Oppressed, ill-used, she faded young,
  And died of grief by slow decay.
Open that casket—look how bright
Those jewels flash upon the sight;
The brilliants have not lost a ray
Of lustre since her wedding-day.
But see—upon that pearly chain—
How dim lies Time's discolouring stain!
I've seen that by her daughter worn:
For, ere she died, a child was born;—
A child that ne'er its mother knew,
That lone and almost friendless grew;

For, ever, when its step drew nigh,
Averted was the father's eye;
And then a life impure and wild
Made him a stranger to his child:
Absorbed in vice, he little cared
On what she did, or how she fared.
The love withheld she never sought,
She grew uncherished—learnt untaught;
To her the inward life of thought
Full soon was open laid.
I know not if her friendlessness
Did sometimes on her spirit press,
But plaint she never made.
The book-shelves were her darling treas-
ure,
She rarely seemed the time to measure
While she could read alone.
And she, too, loved the twilight wood,
And often, in her mother's mood,
Away to yonder hill would hie,
Like her, to watch the setting sun,
Or see the stars born, one by one,
Out of the darkening sky.
Nor would she leave that hill till night
Trembled from pole to pole with light;

Even then, upon her homeward way,
Long—long her wandering steps delayed
To quit the sombre forest shade,
Through which her eerie pathway lay.
You ask if she had beauty's grace?
I know not—but a nobler face
My eyes have seldom seen;
A keen and fine intelligence,
And, better still, the truest sense
Were in her speaking mien.
But bloom or lustre was there none,
Only at moments fitful shone
An ardour in her eye,
That kindled on her cheek a flush,
Warm as a red sky's passing blush
And quick with energy.
Her speech, too, was not common speech,
No wish to shine, or aim to teach,
Was in her words displayed:
She still began with quiet sense,
But oft the force of eloquence
Came to her lips in aid;

Language and voice unconscious changed,
And thoughts, in other words arranged,
  Her fervid soul transfused
Into the hearts of those who heard,
And transient strength and ardour stirred
  In minds to strength unused :
Yet in gay crowd or festal glare,
Grave and retiring was her air ;
'Twas seldom, save with me alone,
That fire of feeling freely shone ;
She loved not awe's nor wonder's gaze,
Nor even exaggerated praise,
Nor even notice, if too keen
The curious gazer searched her mien.
Nature's own green expanse revealed
The world, the pleasures she could prize ;
On free hill-side, in sunny field,
In quiet spots by woods concealed
Grew wild and fresh her chosen joys—
  Yet Nature's feelings deeply lay
In that endowed and youthful frame ;
  Shrined in her heart and hid from day,
They burned unseen with silent flame.

In youth's first search for mental light,
She lived but to reflect and learn,
But soon her mind's maturer might
For stronger task did pant, and yearn;
And stronger task did fate assign,
Task that a giant's strength might strain;
To suffer long, and ne'er repine,
Be calm in frenzy, smile at pain.

Pale with the secret war of feeling,
Sustained with courage, mute yet high,
The wounds at which she bled revealing
Only by altered cheek and eye;

She bore in silence—but when passion
Surged in her soul with ceaseless foam,
The storm at last brought desolation,
And drove her exiled from her home.

And silent still, she straight assembled
The wrecks of strength her soul retained;
For though the wasted body trembled,
The unconquered mind to quail disdained.

She crossed the sea—now lone she wanders
By Seine's, or Rhine's, or Arno's flow:
Fain would I know if distance renders
Relief or comfort to her woe.

Fain would I know if, henceforth, ever,
These eyes shall read in hers again,
That light of love which faded never,
Though dimmed so long with secret pain.

She will return, but cold and altered,
Like all whose hopes too soon depart;
Like all on whom have beat, unsheltered,
The bitter blasts that blight the heart.

No more shall I behold her lying
Calm on a pillow, smoothed by me;
No more that spirit, worn with sighing,
Will know the rest of infancy.

If still the paths of lore she follow,
'Twill be with tired and goaded will;
She'll only toil, the aching hollow,
The joyless blank of life to fill.

And oh! full oft, quite spent and weary,
Her hand will pause, her head decline;
That labour seems so hard and dreary,
On which no ray of hope may shine.

Thus the pale blight of time and sorrow
Will shade with grey her soft, dark hair;
Then comes the day that knows no morrow,
And death succeeds to long despair.

So speaks experience, sage and hoary;
I see it plainly, know it well,
Like one who, having read a story,
Each incident therein can tell.

Touch not that ring; 'twas his, the
sire
Of that forsaken child;
And nought his relics can inspire
Save memories sin-defiled.

I, who sat by his wife's death-bed,
I, who his daughter loved,
Could almost curse the guilty dead,
For woes the guiltless proved.

And heaven did curse—they found him
laid,
When crime for wrath was ripe,
Cold—with the suicidal blade
Clutched in his desperate gripe.

'Twas near that long-deserted hut,
Which in the wood decays,
Death's axe, self-wielded, struck his
root,
And lopped his desperate days.

You know the spot, where three black
trees,
Lift up their branches fell,
And moaning, ceaseless as the seas,
Still seem, in every passing breeze,
The deed of blood to tell.

They named him mad, and laid his
bones
Where holier ashes lie;
Yet doubt not that his spirit groans
In hell's eternity.

But, lo! night, closing o'er the earth,
Infects our thoughts with gloom;
Come, let us strive to rally mirth
Where glows a clear and tranquil hearth
In some more cheerful room.

THE WIFE'S WILL.

SIT still—a word—a breath may break
(As light airs stir a sleeping lake)
The glassy calm that soothes my woes—
The sweet, the deep, the full repose.
O leave me not! for ever be
Thus, more than life itself to me!

Yes, close beside thee let me kneel—
Give me thy hand, that I may feel
The friend so true—so tried—so dear,
My heart's own chosen indeed is near;
And check me not—this hour divine
Belongs to me—is fully mine.

'Tis thy own hearth thou sitt'st beside,
After long absence—wandering wide;
'Tis thy own wife reads in thine eyes
A promise clear of stormless skies;

For faith and true love light the rays
Which shine responsive to her gaze.

Ay,—well that single tear may fall;
Ten thousand might mine eyes recall,
Which from their lids ran blinding
fast,
In hours of grief, yet scarcely past;
Well may'st thou speak of love to me,
For, Oh! most truly—I love thee!

Yet smile—for we are happy now.
Whence, then, that sadness on thy
brow?
What sayest thou? "We must once
again,
Ere long, be severed by the main!"
I knew not this—I deemed no more
Thy step would err from Britain's shore.

"Duty commands!" 'Tis true—'tis
just;
Thy slightest word I wholly trust,
Nor by request, nor faintest sigh,
Would I to turn thy purpose try;

But, William, hear my solemn vow—
Hear and confirm!—with thee I go.

"Distance and suffering," didst thou say?
"Danger by night, and toil by day?"
Oh, idle words and vain are these;
Hear me! I cross with thee the seas.
Such risk as thou must meet and dare,
I—thy true wife—will duly share.

Passive, at home, I will not pine;
Thy toils, thy perils shall be mine;
Grant this—and be hereafter paid
By a warm heart's devoted aid:
'Tis granted—with that yielding kiss,
Entered my soul unmingled bliss.

Thanks, William, thanks! thy love has joy,
Pure, undefiled with base alloy!
'Tis not a passion, false and blind,
Inspires, enchains, absorbs my mind;
Worthy, I feel, art thou to be
Loved with *my* perfect energy.

This evening now shall sweetly flow,
Lit by our clear fire's happy glow;
And parting's peace-embittering fear
Is warned our hearts to come not near;
For fate admits my soul's decree,
In bliss or bale—to go with thee!

THE WOOD.

BUT two miles more, and then we rest!
  Well, there is still an hour of day,
And long the brightness of the West
  Will light us on our devious way;
Sit then, awhile, here in this wood—
So total is the solitude,
    We safely may delay.

These massive roots afford a seat,
  Which seems for weary travellers made.
There rest. The air is soft and sweet
  In this sequestered forest glade,
And there are scents of flowers around,
The evening dew draws from the ground;
    How soothingly they spread!

Yes ; I was tired, but not at heart ;
No—that beats full of sweet content,
For now I have my natural part
Of action with adventure blent ;
Cast forth on the wide world with thee,
And all my once waste energy
To weighty purpose bent.

Yet — say'st thou, spies around us roam,
Our aims are termed conspiracy ?
Haply, no more our English home
An anchorage for us may be ?
That there is risk our mutual blood
May redden in some lonely wood
The knife of treachery ?

Say'st thou, that where we lodge each night,
In each lone farm, or lonelier hall
Of Norman Peer—ere morning light
Suspicion must as duly fall,
As day returns—such vigilance
Presides and watches over France,
Such rigour governs all ?

I fear not, William; dost thou fear?
So that the knife does not divide,
It may be ever hovering near:
I could not tremble at thy side,
And strenuous love—like mine for thee—
Is buckler strong 'gainst treachery,
And turns its stab aside.

I am resolved that thou shalt learn
To trust my strength as I trust thine;
I am resolved our souls shall burn
With equal, steady, mingling shine;
Part of the field is conquered now,
Our lives in the same channel flow,
Along the self-same line;

And while no groaning storm is heard,
Thou seem'st content it should be so,
But soon as comes a warning word
Of danger—straight thine anxious brow
Bends over me a mournful shade,
As doubting if my powers are made
To ford the floods of woe.

Know, then it is my spirit swells,
And drinks, with eager joy, the air
Of freedom—where at last it dwells,
Chartered, a common task to share
With thee, and then it stirs alert,
And pants to learn what menaced hurt
Demands for thee its care.

Remember, I have crossed the deep,
And stood with thee on deck, to gaze
On waves that rose in threatening heap,
While stagnant lay a heavy haze,
Dimly confusing sea with sky,
And baffling, even, the pilot's eye,
Intent to thread the maze—

Of rocks, on Bretagne's dangerous coast,
And find a way to steer our band
To the one point obscure, which lost,
Flung us, as victims, on the strand ;—
All, elsewhere, gleamed the Gallic sword,
And not a wherry could be moored
Along the guarded land.

I feared not then—I fear not now;
  The interest of each stirring scene
Wakes a new sense, a welcome glow,
  In every nerve and bounding vein;
Alike on turbid Channel sea,
Or in still wood of Normandy,
    I feel as born again.

The rain descended that wild morn
  When, anchoring in the cove at last,
Our band, all weary and forlorn,
  Ashore, like wave-worn sailors, cast
Sought for a sheltering roof in vain,
And scarce could scanty food obtain
    To break their morning fast.

Thou didst thy crust with me divide,
  Thou didst thy cloak around me fold;
And, sitting silent by thy side,
  I ate the bread in peace untold:
Given kindly from thy hand, 'twas sweet
As costly fare or princely treat
    On royal plate of gold.

Sharp blew the sleet upon my face,
  And, rising wild, the gusty wind
Drove on those thundering waves apace,
  Our crew so late had left behind;
But, spite of frozen shower and storm,
So close to thee, my heart beat warm,
    And tranquil slept my mind.

So now—nor foot-sore nor opprest
  With walking all this August day,
I taste a heaven in this brief rest,
  This gipsy-halt beside the way.
England's wild flowers are fair to view,
Like balm is England's summer dew,
    Like gold her sunset ray.

But the white violets, growing here,
  Are sweeter than I yet have seen,
And ne'er did dew so pure and clear
  Distil on forest mosses green,
As now, called forth by summer heat,
Perfumes our cool and fresh retreat—
    These fragrant limes between.

That sunset! Look beneath the boughs,
  Over the copse—beyond the hills;
How soft, yet deep and warm, it glows,
  And heaven with rich suffusion fills;
With hues where still the opal's tint,
Its gleam of prisoned fire, is blent,
    Where flame through azure thrills!

Depart we now—for fast will fade
  That solemn splendour of decline,
And deep must be the after-shade,
  As stars alone to-night will shine;
No moon is destined pale to gaze
On such a day's vast phœnix blaze,
    A day in fires decayed!

There hand-in-hand we tread again
  The mazes of this varying wood,
And soon, amid a cultured plain,
  Girt in with fertile solitude,
We shall our resting-place descry,
Marked by one roof-tree; towering high
    Above a farmstead rude.

Refreshed, ere long, with rustic fare,
  We'll seek a couch of dreamless ease;
Courage will guard thy heart from fear,
  And Love give mine divinest peace:
To-morrow brings more dangerous toil,
And through its conflict and turmoil
    We'll pass, as God shall please.

[The preceding composition refers, doubtless, to the scenes acted in France during the last year of the Consulate.]

FRANCES.

SHE will not sleep, for fear of dreams,
But, rising, quits her restless bed,
And walks where some beclouded beams
Of moonlight through the hall are shed.

Obedient to the goad of grief,
Her steps, now fast, now lingering slow,
In varying motion seek relief
From the Eumenides of woe.

Wringing her hands, at intervals—
But long as mute as phantom dim—
She glides along the dusky walls,
Under the black oak rafters grim.

The close air of the grated tower
  Stifles a heart that scarce can beat,
And, though so late and lone the hour,
  Forth pass her wandering, faltering
    feet;

And on the pavement, spread before
  The long front of the mansion grey,
Her steps imprint the night-frost hoar,
  Which pale on grass and granite
    lay.

Not long she stayed where misty moon
  And shimmering stars could on her
    look,
But through the garden archway soon
  Her strange and gloomy path she
    took.

Some firs, coëval with the tower,
  Their straight black boughs stretched
    o'er her head;
Unseen, beneath this sable bower,
  Rustled her dress and rapid tread.

There was an alcove in that shade,
Screening a rustic seat and stand;
Weary she sat her down, and laid
Her hot brow on her burning hand.

To solitude and to the night
Some words she now, in murmurs, said;
And trickling through her fingers white,
Some tears of misery she shed.

"God help me in my grievous need,
God help me in my inward pain;
Which cannot ask for pity's meed,
Which has no license to complain;

"Which must be borne; yet who can bear
Hours long, days long, a constant weight—
The yoke of absolute despair,
A suffering wholly desolate?

"Who can for ever crush the heart,
Restrain its throbbing, curb its life?
Dissemble truth with ceaseless art,
With outward calm mask inward strife?"

She waited—as for some reply
The still and cloudy night gave none;
Ere long, with deep-drawn, trembling sigh,
Her heavy plaint again begun.

"Unloved—I love; unwept—I weep;
Grief I restrain—hope I repress:
Vain is this anguish—fixed and deep;
Vainer desires and dreams of bliss:

"My love awakes no love again,
My tears collect, and fall unfelt;
My sorrow touches none with pain,
My humble hopes to nothing melt.

"For me the universe is dumb,
Stone-deaf, and blank, and wholly blind;
Life I must bound, existence sum
In the strait limits of one mind;

"That mind my own. Oh! narrow cell;
Dark—imageless—a living tomb!
There must I sleep, there wake and dwell
Content, with palsy, pain, and gloom."

Again she paused; a moan of pain,
A stifled sob, alone was heard;
Long silence followed—then again
Her voice the stagnant midnight stirred:

"Must it be so? Is this my fate?
Can I nor struggle, nor contend?
And am I doomed for years to wait,
Watching death's lingering axe descend?

"And when it falls, and when I die,
What follows? Vacant nothingness?
The blank of lost identity?
Erasure both of pain and bliss?

"I've heard of heaven—I would believe;
For if this earth indeed be all,
Who longest lives may deepest grieve;
Most blest, whom sorrows soonest call.

"Oh! leaving disappointment here,
Will man find hope on yonder coast?
Hope, which on earth shines never clear,
And oft in clouds is wholly lost.

"Will he hope's source of light behold,
Fruition's spring, where doubts expire;
And drink, in waves of living gold,
Contentment, full, for long desire?

"Will he find bliss, which here he
dreamed?
Rest, which was weariness on earth?
Knowledge, which, if o'er life it
beamed,
Served but to prove it void of
worth?

"Will he find love without lust's leaven,
Love fearless, tearless, perfect, pure,
To all with equal bounty given;
In all, unfeigned, unfailing, sure?

"Will he, from penal sufferings free,
Released from shroud and wormy
clod,
All calm and glorious, rise and see
Creation's Sire—Existence's God?

"Then, glancing back on Time's brief
woes,
Will he behold them, fading, fly;
Swept from Eternity's repose,
Like sullying cloud from pure blue
sky?

"If so, endure, my weary frame ;
And when thy anguish strikes too deep,
And when all troubled burns life's flame,
Think of the quiet, final sleep ;

"Think of the glorious waking-hour,
Which will not dawn on grief and tears,
But on a ransomed spirit's power,
Certain and free from mortal fears.

"Seek now thy couch, and lie till morn,
Then from thy chamber, calm, descend,
With mind nor tossed, nor anguish-torn,
But tranquil, fixed, to wait the end.

"And when thy opening eyes shall see
Mementos on the chamber wall,
Of one who has forgotten thee,
Shed not the tear of acrid gall.

"The tear which, welling from the heart,
Burns where its drop corrosive falls,
And makes each nerve in torture start,
At feelings it too well recalls :

"When the sweet hope of being loved
Threw Eden sunshine on life's way ;
When every sense and feeling proved
Expectancy of brightest day ·

"When the hand trembled to receive
A thrilling clasp, which seemed so near,
And the heart ventured to believe
Another heart esteemed it dear :

"When words, half love, all tenderness,
Were hourly heard, as hourly spoken,
When the long sunny days of bliss
Only by moonlight nights were broken :

"Till, drop by drop, the cup of joy,
Filled full, with purple light was glowing,
And Faith, which watched it sparkling high,
Still never dreamt the overflowing.

"It fell not with a sudden crashing,
It poured not out like open sluice;
No, sparkling still, and redly flashing,
Drained, drop by drop, the generous juice.

"I saw it sink, and strove to taste it—
My eager lips approached the brim;
The movement only seemed to waste it—
It sank to dregs, all harsh and dim.

"These I have drunk, and they for ever
Have poisoned life and love for me;
A draught from Sodom's lake could never
More fiery, salt, and bitter be.

"Oh! Love was all a thin illusion,
Joy but the desert's flying stream;
And, glancing back on long delusion,
My memory grasps a hollow dream.

"Yet whence that wondrous change of feeling,
I never knew, and cannot learn;
Nor why my lover's eye, congealing,
Grew cold and clouded, proud and stern.

"Nor wherefore, friendship's forms forgetting,
He careless left, and cool withdrew,
Nor spoke of grief nor fond regretting,
Nor ev'n one glance of comfort threw.

"And neither word nor token sending,
Of kindness, since the parting day,
His course, for distant regions bending,
Went, self-contained and calm, away.

"O bitter, blighting, keen sensation,
Which will not weaken, cannot die,
Hasten thy work of desolation,
And let my tortured spirit fly!

"Vain as the passing gale, my crying;
Though lightning-struck, I must live on;
I know at heart there is no dying
Of love, and ruined hope, alone.

"Still strong and young, and warm with vigour,
Though scathed, I long shall greenly grow;
And many a storm of wildest rigour
Shall yet break o'er my shivered bough.

"Rebellious now to blank inertion,
My unused strength demands a task;
Travel, and toil, and full exertion
Are the last, only boon I ask.

"Whence, then, this vain and barren dreaming
Of death, and dubious life to come?
I see a nearer beacon gleaming
Over dejection's sea of gloom.

"The very wildness of my sorrow
Tells me I yet have innate force;
My track of life has been too narrow,
Effort shall trace a broader course.

"The world is not in yonder tower,
Earth is not prisoned in that room,
Mid whose dark panels, hour by hour,
I've sat, the slave and prey of gloom.

"One feeling—turned to utter anguish,
Is not my being's only aim;
When, lorn and loveless, life will languish,
But courage can revive the flame.

"He, when he left me, went a-roving
To sunny climes beyond the sea;
And I, the weight of woe removing,
Am free and fetterless as he.

"New scenes, new language, skies less clouded,
May once more wake the wish to live;
Strange foreign towns, astir and crowded,
New pictures to the mind may give.

"New forms and faces, passing ever,
May hide the one I still retain,
Defined and fixed, and fading never,
Stamped deep on vision, heart, and brain.

"And we might meet—time may have changed him;
Chance may reveal the mystery,
The secret influence which estranged him;
Love may restore him yet to me.

"False thought—false hope—in scorn
be banished!
I am not loved, nor loved have
been;
Recall not, then, the dreams scarce
vanished;
Traitors! mislead me not again!

"To words like yours I bid defiance,
'Tis such my mental wreck have
made;
Of God alone, and self-reliance,
I ask for solace—hope for aid.

"Morn comes, and ere meridian glory
O'er these, my natal woods shall
smile,
Both lonely wood and mansion hoary
I'll leave behind, full many a mile."

GILBERT.

I.—THE GARDEN.

ABOVE the city hung the moon,
  Right o'er a plot of ground
Where flowers and orchard-trees were
    fenced
  With lofty walls around :
'Twas Gilbert's garden. There to-night
  Awhile he walked alone ;
And, tired with sedentary toil,
  Mused where the moonlight shone.

This garden, in a city heart,
  Lay still as houseless wild,
Though many-windowed mansion fronts
  Were round it closely piled ;
But thick their walls, and those within
  Lived lives by noise unstirred ;
Like wafting of an angel's wing,
  Time's flight by them was heard.

Some soft piano-notes alone
  Were sweet as faintly given,
Where ladies, doubtless, cheered the hearth
  With song that winter-even.
The city's many-mingled sounds
  Rose like the hum of ocean;
They rather lulled the heart than roused
  Its pulse to faster motion.

Gilbert has paced the single walk
  An hour, yet is not weary;
And, though it be a winter night,
  He feels nor cold nor dreary.
The prime of life is in his veins,
  And sends his blood fast flowing,
And Fancy's fervour warms the thoughts
  Now in his bosom glowing.

Those thoughts recur to early love,
  Or what he love would name,
Though haply Gilbert's secret deeds
  Might other title claim.

Such theme not oft his mind absorbs,
He to the world clings fast,
And too much for the present lives,
To linger o'er the past.

But now the evening's deep repose
Has glided to his soul;
That moonlight falls on Memory,
And shows her fading scroll.
One name appears in every line
The gentle rays shine o'er,
And still he smiles and still repeats
That one name—Elinor.

There is no sorrow in his smile,
No kindness in his tone;
The triumph of a selfish heart
Speaks coldly there alone.
He says: "She loved me more than life;
And truly it was sweet
To see so fair a woman kneel
In bondage at my feet.

"There was a sort of quiet bliss
To be so deeply loved,
To gaze on trembling eagerness
And sit myself unmoved ;
And when it pleased my pride to grant
At last some rare caress,
To feel the fever of that hand
My fingers deigned to press.

"'Twas sweet to see her strive to hide
What every glance revealed ;
Endowed, the while, with despot-might
Her destiny to wield.
I knew myself no perfect man,
Nor, as she deemed, divine ;
I knew that I was glorious—but
By her reflected shine ;

"Her youth, her native energy,
Her powers new-born and fresh—
'Twas these with Godhead sanctified
My sensual frame of flesh.

Yet, like a god did I descend
  At last to meet her love ;
And, like a god, I then withdrew
  To my own heaven above.

" And never more could she invoke
  My presence to her sphere ;
No prayer, no plaint, no cry of hers
  Could win my awful ear.
I knew her blinded constancy
  Would ne'er my deeds betray,
And, calm in conscience, whole in heart,
  I went my tranquil way.

" Yet, sometimes, I still feel a wish,
  The fond and flattering pain
Of passion's anguish to create
  In her young breast again.
Bright was the lustre of her eyes
  When they caught fire from mine ;
If I had power—this very hour,
  Again I'd light their shine.

"But where she is, or how she lives,
I have no clue to know;
I've heard she long my absence pined,
And left her home in woe.
But busied, then, in gathering gold,
As I am busied now,
I could not turn from such pursuit,
To weep a broken vow.

"Nor could I give to fatal risk
The fame I ever prized;
Even now, I fear, that precious fame
Is too much compromised."
An inward trouble dims his eye,
Some riddle he would solve;
Some method to unloose a knot,
His anxious thoughts revolve.

He, pensive, leans against a tree,
A leafy evergreen—
The boughs, the moonlight, intercept,
And hide him like a screen;

He starts—the tree shakes with his tremor,
Yet nothing near him pass'd;
He hurries up the garden alley
In strangely sudden haste.

With shaking hands he lifts the latchet,
Steps o'er the threshold stone;
The heavy door slips from his fingers—
It shuts, and he is gone.
What touched, transfixed, appalled his soul?—
A nervous thought, no more;
'Twill sink like stone in placid pool,
And calm close smoothly o'er.

II.—THE PARLOR.

Warm is the parlor atmosphere,
Serene the lamp's soft light;
The vivid embers, red and clear,
Proclaim a frosty night.

Books, varied, on the table lie,
  Three children o'er them bend,
And all, with curious, eager eye,
  The turning leaf attend.

Picture and tale alternately
  Their simple hearts delight,
And interest deep, and tempered glee,
  Illume their aspects bright.
The parents, from their fireside place,
  Behold that pleasant scene,
And joy is on the mother's face,
  Pride in the father's mien.

As Gilbert sees his blooming wife,
  Beholds his children fair,
No thought has he of transient strife,
  Or past though piercing fear.
The voice of happy infancy
  Lisps sweetly in his ear,
His wife, with pleased and peaceful eye,
  Sits, kindly smiling, near.

The fire glows on her silken dress,
And shows its ample grace,
And warmly tints each hazel tress,
Curled soft around her face.
The beauty that in youth he wooed
Is beauty still, unfaded;
The brow of ever placid mood
No churlish grief has shaded.

Prosperity, in Gilbert's home,
Abides the guest of years;
There Want or Discord never come,
And seldom Toil or Tears.
The carpets bear the peaceful print
Of comfort's velvet tread,
And golden gleams, from plenty sent,
In every nook are shed.

The very silken spaniel seems
Of quiet ease to tell,
As near its mistress' feet it dreams,
Sunk in a cushion's swell;

And smiles seem native to the eyes
  Of those sweet children three ;
They have but looked on tranquil
    skies,
  And know not misery.

Alas ! that Misery should come
  In such an hour as this ;
Why could she not so calm a home
  A little longer miss ?
But she is now within the door,
  Her steps advancing glide ;
Her sullen shade has crossed the floor,
  She stands at Gilbert's side.

She lays her hand upon his heart,
  It bounds with agony ;
His fireside chair shakes with the start
  That shook the garden tree.
His wife towards the children looks,
  She does not mark his mien ;
The children, bending o'er their books,
  His terror have not seen.

In his own home, by his own hearth,
  He sits in solitude,
And circled round with light and mirth,
  Cold horror chills his blood.
His mind would hold with desperate clutch
  The scene that round him lies;
No—changed, as by some wizard's touch,
  The present prospect flies.

A tumult vague—a viewless strife
  His futile struggles crush;
'Twixt him and his an unknown life
  And unknown feelings rush.
He sees—but scarce can language paint
  The tissue fancy weaves;
For words oft give but echo faint
  Of thoughts the mind conceives.

Noise, tumult strange, and darkness dim
  Efface both light and quiet;
No shape is in those shadows grim,
  No voice in that wild riot.

Sustain'd and strong, a wondrous blast
  Above and round him blows ;
A greenish gloom, dense overcast,
  Each moment denser grows.

He nothing knows—nor clearly sees,
  Resistance checks his breath,
The high, impetuous, ceaseless breeze
  Blows on him cold as death.
And still the undulating gloom
  Mocks sight with formless motion :
Was such sensation Jonah's doom,
  Gulphed in the depths of ocean ?

Streaking the air, the nameless vision,
  Fast-driven, deep-sounding, flows ;
Oh ! whence its source, and what its mission ?
  How will its terrors close ?
Long-sweeping, rushing, vast and void,
  The universe it swallows ;
And still the dark, devouring tide
  A typhoon tempest follows.

More slow it rolls; its furious race
Sinks to its solemn gliding;
The stunning roar, the wind's wild chase,
To stillness are subsiding;
And, slowly borne along, a form
The shapeless chaos varies;
Poised in the eddy to the storm,
Before the eye it tarries:

A woman drowned — sunk in the deep,
On a long wave reclining;
The circling waters' crystal sweep,
Like glass, her shape enshrining.
Her pale dead face, to Gilbert turned,
Seems as in sleep reposing;
A feeble light, now first discerned,
The features well disclosing.

No effort from the haunted air
The ghastly scene could banish;
That hovering wave, arrested there,
Rolled—throbbed—but did not vanish.

If Gilbert upward turned his gaze,
He saw the ocean-shadow;
If he looked down, the endless seas
Lay green as summer meadow.

And straight before, the pale corpse lay,
Upborne by air or billow,
So near, he could have touched the spray
That churned around its pillow.
The hollow anguish of the face
Had moved a fiend to sorrow;
Not death's fixed calm could rase the trace
Of suffering's deep-worn furrow.

All moved; a strong returning blast,
The mass of waters raising,
Bore wave and passive carcase past,
While Gilbert yet was gazing.
Deep in her isle-conceiving womb
It seemed the ocean thundered,
And soon, by realms of rushing gloom,
Were seer and phantom sundered.

Then swept some timbers from a
wreck,
On following surges riding;
Then seaweed, in the turbid rack
Uptorn, went slowly gliding.
The horrid shade, by slow degrees,
A beam of light defeated,
And then the roar of raving seas,
Fast, far, and faint, retreated.

And all was gone—gone like a mist,
Corse, billows, tempest, wreck;
Three children close to Gilbert prest
And clung around his neck.
"Good night! good night!" the prattlers said,
And kissed their father's cheek;
'Twas now the hour their quiet
bed
And placid rest to seek.

The mother with her offspring goes
To hear their evening prayer;
She nought of Gilbert's vision knows,
And nought of his despair.

Yet, pitying God, abridge the time
Of anguish, now his fate!
Though, haply, great has been his crime,
Thy mercy, too, is great.

Gilbert, at length, uplifts his head,
Bent for some moments low,
And there is neither grief nor dread
Upon his subtle brow.
For well can he his feelings task,
And well his looks command;
His features well his heart can mask,
With smiles and smoothness bland.

Gilbert has reasoned with his mind—
He says 'twas all a dream;
He strives his inward sight to blind
Against truth's inward beam.
He pitied not that shadowy thing,
When it was flesh and blood;
Nor now can pity's balmy spring
Refresh his arid mood.

"And if that dream has spoken truth,"
Thus musingly he says;
"If Elinor be dead, in sooth,
Such chance the shock repays:
A net was woven round my feet,
I scarce could further go;
Ere shame had forced a fast retreat,
Dishonour brought me low.

"Conceal her, then, deep, silent sea,
Give her a secret grave!
She sleeps in peace, and I am free,
No longer terror's slave:
And homage still, from all the world,
Shall greet my spotless name,
Since surges break and waves are curled
Above its threatened shame."

III.—THE WELCOME HOME.

Above the city hangs the moon,
Some clouds are boding rain;
Gilbert, erewhile on journey gone,
To-night comes home again.

Ten years have passed above his head,
  Each year has brought him gain;
His prosperous life has smoothly sped,
  Without or tear or stain.

'Tis somewhat late—the city clocks
  Twelve deep vibrations toll,
As Gilbert at the portal knocks,
  Which is his journey's goal.
The street is still and desolate,
  The moon hid by a cloud;
Gilbert, impatient, will not wait—
  His second knock peals loud.

The clocks are hushed—there's not a
    light
  In any window nigh,
And not a single planet bright
  Looks from the clouded sky;
The air is raw, the rain descends,
  A bitter north-wind blows;
His cloak the traveller scarce defends—
  Will not the door unclose?

He knocks the third time, and the
last;
His summons now they hear:
Within, a footstep, hurrying fast,
Is heard approaching near.
The bolt is drawn, the clanking chain
Falls to the floor of stone;
And Gilbert to his heart will strain
His wife and children soon.

The hand that lifts the latchet, holds
A candle to his sight,
And Gilbert, on the step, beholds
A woman clad in white.
Lo! water from her dripping dress
Runs on the streaming floor;
From every dark and clinging tress
The drops incessant pour.

There's none but her to welcome him;
She holds the candle high,
And, motionless in form and limb,
Stands cold and silent nigh;

There's sand and seaweed on her robe,
  Her hollow eyes are blind;
No pulse in such a frame can throb,
  No life is there defined.

Gilbert turned ashy-white, but still
  His lips vouchsafed no cry;
He spurred his strength and master-
    will
  To pass the figure by,—
But, moving slow, it faced him straight,
  It would not flinch nor quail:
Then first did Gilbert's strength abate,
  His stony firmness fail.

He sank upon his knees and prayed;
  The shape stood rigid there;
He called aloud for human aid,
  No human aid was near.
An accent strange did thus repeat
  Heaven's stern but just decree:
"The measure thou to her didst mete,
    To thee shall measured be!"

Gilbert sprang from his bended knees,
By the pale spectre pushed,
And, wild as one whom demons seize,
Up the hall-staircase rushed;
Entered his chamber—near the bed
Sheathed steel and firearms hung—
Impelled by maniac purpose dread
He chose those stores among.

Across his throat a keen-edged knife
With vigorous hand he drew;
The wound was wide—his outraged life
Rushed rash and redly through.
And thus died, by a shameful death,
A wise and worldly man,
Who never drew but selfish breath
Since first his life began.

LIFE.

LIFE, believe, is not a dream
  So dark as sages say;
Oft a little morning rain
  Foretells a pleasant day.
Sometimes there are clouds of gloom,
  But these are transient all;
If the shower will make the roses bloom,
  Oh, why lament its fall?
    Rapidly, merrily,
  Life's sunny hours flit by,
    Gratefully, cheerily,
  Enjoy them as they fly!

What though Death at times steps in,
  And calls our best away?
What though sorrow seems to win,
  O'er hope, a heavy sway?

Yet Hope again elastic springs,
  Unconquered, though she fell;
Still buoyant are her golden wings,
  Still strong to bear us well.
    Manfully, fearlessly,
  The day of trial bear,
    For gloriously, victoriously,
  Can courage quell despair!

THE LETTER.

WHAT is she writing? Watch her now,
  How fast her fingers move!
How eagerly her youthful brow
  Is bent in thought above!

Her long curls, drooping, shade the light,
  She puts them quick aside,
Nor knows that band of crystals bright
  Her hasty touch untied.
It slips adown her silken dress,
  Falls glittering at her feet;
Unmarked it falls, for she no less
  Pursues her labour sweet.

The very loveliest hour that shines
  Is in that deep blue sky;
The golden sun of June declines,
  It has not caught her eye.

The cheerful lawn, and unclosed gate,
  The white road, far away,
In vain for her light footsteps wait,
  She comes not forth to-day.
There is an open door of glass
  Close by that lady's chair,
From thence, to slopes of mossy grass,
  Descends a marble stair.

Tall plants of bright and spicy bloom
  Around the threshold grow;
Their leaves and blossoms shade the room
  From that sun's deepening glow.
Why does she not a moment glance
  Between the clustering flowers,
And mark in heaven the radiant dance
  Of evening's rosy hours?
Oh, look again! Still fixed her eye,
  Unsmiling, earnest, still,
And fast her pen and fingers fly,
  Urged by her eager will.

Her soul is in th' absorbing task;
  To whom, then, doth she write?
Nay, watch her still more closely, ask
  Her own eyes' serious light;
Where do they turn, as now her pen
  Hangs o'er th' unfinished line?
Whence fell the tearful gleam that then
  Did in their dark spheres shine?
The summer-parlor looks so dark,
  When from that sky you turn,
And from th' expanse of that green park
  You scarce may aught discern.

Yet o'er the piles of porcelain rare,
  O'er flower-stand, couch, and vase,
Sloped, as if leaning on the air,
  One picture meets the gaze.
'Tis there she turns; you may not see,
  Distinct, what form defines
The clouded mass of mystery
  Yon broad gold frame confines.
But look again; inured to shade
  Your eyes now faintly trace
A stalwart form, a massive head,
  A firm, determined face.

Black Spanish locks, a sunburnt cheek,
  A brow high, broad, and white,
Where every furrow seems to speak
  Of mind and moral might.
Is that her god? I cannot tell;
  Her eye a moment met
Th' impending picture, then it fell
  Darkened and dimmed and wet.
A moment more, her task is done,
  And sealed the letter lies;
And now, towards the setting sun
  She turns her tearful eyes.

Those tears flow over, wonder not,
  For by the inscription see
In what a strange and distant spot
  Her heart of hearts must be!
Three seas and many a league of land
  That letter must pass o'er,
Ere read by him to whose loved hand
  'Tis sent from England's shore.
Remote colonial wilds detain
  Her husband, loved though stern;
She, mid that smiling English scene,
  Weeps for his wished return.

REGRET.

LONG ago I wished to leave
  "The house where I was born;"
Long ago I used to grieve,
  My home seemed so forlorn.
In other years, its silent rooms
  Were filled with haunting fears;
Now their very memory comes
  O'ercharged with tender tears.

Life and marriage I have known,
  Things once deemed so bright;
Now how utterly is flown
  Every ray of light!
Mid the unknown sea of life
  I no blest isle have found;
At last, through all its wild waves strife,
  My bark is homeward bound.

Farewell, dark and rolling deep!
  Farewell, foreign shore!
Open, in unclouded sweep,
  Thou glorious realm before!
Yet, though I had safely pass'd
  That weary, vexed main,
One loved voice, through surge and
      blast,
  Could call me back again.

Though the soul's bright morning rose
  O'er Paradise for me,
William! even from Heaven's repose
  I'd turn, invoked by thee!
Storm nor surge should e'er arrest
  My soul, exulting then:
All my heaven was once thy breast,
  Would it were mine again!

PRESENTIMENT.

"SISTER, you've sat there all the day,
Come to the hearth awhile;
The wind so wildly sweeps away,
The clouds so darkly pile.
That open book has lain, unread,
For hours upon your knee;
You've never smiled nor turned your head;
What can you, sister, see?"

"Come hither, Jane, look down the field;
How dense a mist creeps on!
The path, the hedge, are both concealed,
Ev'n the white gate is gone;
No landscape through the fog I trace,
No hill with pastures green;
All featureless is Nature's face,
All masked in clouds her mien.

"Scarce is the rustle of a leaf
Heard in our garden now;
The years grow old, its days wax brief,
The tresses leave its brow.
The rain drives fast before the wind,
The sky is blank and grey;
O Jane, what sadness fills the mind
On such a dreary day!"

"You think too much, my sister dear;
You sit too long alone;
What though November days be drear?
Full soon will they be gone.
I've swept the hearth, and placed your chair,
Come, Emma, sit by me;
Our own fireside is never drear,
Though late and wintry wane the year,
Though rough the night may be."

"The peaceful glow of our fireside
Imparts no peace to me:
My thoughts would rather wander wide
Than rest, dear Jane, with thee.

I'm on a distant journey bound,
  And if, about my heart,
Too closely kindred ties were bound,
  'Twould break when forced to part.

"'Soon will November days be o'er:'
  Well have you spoken, Jane:
My own forebodings tell me more—
For me, I know by presage sure,
  They'll ne'er return again:
Ere long, nor sun nor storm to me
  Will bring or joy or gloom;
They reach not that Eternity
  Which soon will be my home."

Eight months are gone, the summer sun
  Sets in a glorious sky;
A quiet field, all green and lone,
  Receives its rosy dye.
Jane sits upon a shaded stile,
  Alone she sits there now;
Her head rests on her hand the while,
  And thought o'ercasts her brow.

She's thinking of one winter's day,
  A few short months ago,
When Emma's bier was borne away
  O'er wastes of frozen snow.
She's thinking how that drifted snow
  Dissolved in spring's first gleam,
And how her sister's memory now
  Fades, even as fades a dream.

The snow will whiten earth again,
  But Emma comes no more ;
She left, mid winter's sleet and rain,
  This world for Heaven's far shore.
On Beulah's hills she wanders now,
  On Eden's tranquil plain ;
To her shall Jane hereafter go,
  She ne'er shall come to Jane !

THE TEACHER'S MONOLOGUE.

THE room is quiet, thoughts alone
  People its mute tranquillity;
The yoke put off, the long task done,—
  I am, as it is bliss to be,
Still and untroubled. Now, I see,
  For the first time, how soft the day
O'er waveless water, stirless tree,
  Silent and sunny, wings its way.
Now, as I watch that distant hill,
  So faint, so blue, so far removed,
Sweet dreams of home my heart may fill,
  That home where I am known and loved:
It lies beyond; yon azure brow
  Parts me from all Earth holds for me;
And, morn and eve, my yearnings flow
  Thitherward tending, changelessly.

My happiest hours, ay! all the time,
I love to keep in memory,
Lapsed among moors, ere life's first prime
Decayed to dark anxiety.

Sometimes, I think a narrow heart
Makes me thus mourn those far away,
And keeps my love so far apart
From friends and friendships of to-day;
Sometimes, I think 'tis but a dream
I treasure up so jealously,
All the sweet thoughts I live on seem
To vanish into vacancy:
And then, this strange, coarse world around
Seems all that's palpable and true;
And every sight and every sound
Combine my spirit to subdue
To aching grief; so void and lone
Is Life, and Earth—so worse than vain,
The hopes that, in my own heart sown,
And cherished by such sun and rain

As Joy and transient Sorrow shed,
  Have ripened to a harvest there :
Alas! methinks I hear it said,
  "Thy golden sheaves are empty air."

All fades away ; my very home
  I think will soon be desolate ;
I hear, at times, a warning come
  Of bitter partings at its gate ;
And, if I should return and see
  The hearth-fire quenched, the vacant
    chair ;
And hear it whispered mournfully,
  That farewells have been spoken
    there,
What shall I do, and whither turn ?
Where look for peace ? When cease to
    mourn ?

'Tis not the air I wished to play,
  The strain I wished to sing ;
My wilful spirit slipped away
  And struck another string.

I neither wanted smile nor tear,
  Bright joy nor bitter woe,
But just a song that sweet and clear,
  Though haply sad, might flow.

A quiet song, to solace me
  When sleep refused to come;
A strain to chase despondency
  When sorrowful for home.
In vain I try; I cannot sing;
  All feels so cold and dead;
No wild distress, no gushing spring
  Of tears in anguish shed;

But all the impatient gloom of one
  Who waits a distant day,
When, some great task of suffering done,
  Repose shall toil repay.
For youth departs, and pleasure flies,
  And life consumes away,
And youth's rejoicing ardour dies
  Beneath this drear delay;

And Patience, weary with her yoke,
  Is yielding to despair,
And Health's elastic spring is broke
  Beneath the strain of care.
Life will be gone ere I have lived;
  Where now is Life's first prime?
I've worked and studied, longed and grieved,
  Through all that rosy time.

To toil, to think, to long, to grieve,—
  Is such my future fate?
The morn was dreary, must the eve
  Be also desolate?
Well, such a life at least makes Death
  A welcome, wished-for friend;
Then, aid me, Reason, Patience, Faith,
  To suffer to the end!

PASSION.

SOME have won a wild delight,
  By daring wilder sorrow ;
Could I gain thy love to-night,
  I'd hazard death to-morrow.

Could the battle-struggle earn
  One kind glance from thine eye,
How this withering heart would burn,
  The heady fight to try !

Welcome nights of broken sleep,
  And days of carnage cold,
Could I deem that thou wouldst weep
  To hear my perils told.

Tell me, if with wandering bands
  I roam full far away,
Wilt thou to those distant lands
  In spirit ever stray ?

Wild, long, a trumpet sounds afar;
  Bid me—bid me go
Where Seik and Briton meet in war,
  On Indian Sutlej's flow.

Blood has dyed the Sutlej's waves
  With scarlet stain, I know;
Indus' borders yawn with graves,
  Yet, command me go!

Though rank and high the holocaust
  Of nations steams to heaven,
Glad I'd join the death-doomed host,
  Were but the mandate given.

Passion's strength should nerve my arm,
  Its ardour stir my life,
Till human force to that dread charm
Should yield and sink in wild alarm,
  Like trees to tempest-strife.

If, hot from war, I seek thy love,
  Darest thou turn aside?
Darest thou then my fire reprove,
  By scorn, and maddening pride?

No—my will shall yet control
  Thy will so high and free,
And love shall tame that haughty soul—
  Yes, tenderest love for me.

I'll read my triumph in thine eyes,
  Behold, and prove the change;
Then leave, perchance, my noble prize,
  Once more in arms to range.

I'd die when all the foam is up,
  The bright wine sparkling high;
Nor wait till in the exhausted cup
  Life's dull dregs only lie.

Then Love thus crowned with sweet re-
    ward,
  Hope blest with fulness large,
I'd mount the saddle, draw the sword
  And perish in the charge!

PREFERENCE.

NOT in scorn do I reprove thee,
Not in pride thy vows I waive,
But, believe, I could not love thee,
Wert thou prince, and I a slave.
These, then, are thine oaths of passion?
This, thy tenderness for me?
Judged, even, by thine own confession,
Thou art steeped in perfidy.
Having vanquished, thou wouldst leave me!
Thus I read thee long ago;
Therefore, dared I not deceive thee,
Even with friendship's gentle show.
Therefore, with impassive coldness
Have I ever met thy gaze;
Though, full oft, with daring boldness,
Thou thine eyes to mine didst raise.

Why that smile? Thou now art deem-
ing
This my coldness all untrue,—
But a mask of frozen seeming,
Hiding secret fires from view.
Touch my hand, thou self-deceiver;
Nay—be calm, for I am so:
Does it burn? Does my lip quiver?
Has mine eye a troubled glow?
Canst thou call a moment's colour
To my forehead—to my cheek?
Canst thou tinge their tranquil pallor
With one flattering, feverish streak?
Am I marble? What! no woman
Could so calm before thee stand?
Nothing living, sentient, human,
Could so coldly take thy hand?
Yes—a sister might, a mother:
My good-will is sisterly:
Dream not, then, I strive to smother
Fires that inly burn for thee.
Rave not, rage not, wrath is fruitless,
Fury cannot change my mind;
I but deem the feeling rootless
Which so whirls in passion's wind.

Can I love? Oh, deeply—truly—
Warmly—fondly—but not thee;
And my love is answered duly,
With an equal energy.
Wouldst thou see thy rival? Hasten,
Draw that curtain soft aside,
Look where yon thick branches chasten
Noon, with shades of eventide.
In that glade, where foliage blending
Forms a green arch overhead,
Sits thy rival, thoughtful bending
O'er a stand with papers spread—
Motionless, his fingers plying
That untired, unresting pen;
Time and tide unnoticed flying,
There he sits—the first of men!
Man of conscience—man of reason;
Stern, perchance, but ever just;
Foe to falsehood, wrong, and treason,
Honour's shield, and virtue's trust!
Worker, thinker, firm defender
Of Heaven's truth, man's liberty;
Soul of iron, proof to slander,
Rock where founders tyranny.

Fame he seeks not—but full surely
  She will seek him, in his home;
This I know, and wait securely
  For the atoning hour to come.
To that man my faith is given,
  Therefore, soldier, cease to sue;
While God reigns in earth and heaven,
  I to him will still be true!

EVENING SOLACE.

THE human heart has hidden treasures,
In secret kept, in silence sealed ;—
The thoughts, the hopes, the dreams, the pleasures,
Whose charms were broken if revealed.
And days may pass in gay confusion,
And nights in rosy riot fly,
While, lost in Fame's or Wealth's illusion,
The memory of the Past may die.

But there are hours of lonely musing,
Such as in evening silence come,
When, soft as birds their pinions closing,
The heart's best feelings gather home.

Then in our souls there seems to languish
  A tender grief that is not woe ;
And thoughts that once wrung groans of anguish,
  Now cause but some mild tears to flow.

And feelings, once as strong as passions,
  Float softly back—a faded dream ;
Our own sharp griefs and wild sensations,
  The tale of others' sufferings seem.
Oh! when the heart is freshly bleeding,
  How longs it for that time to be,
When, through the mist of years receding,
  Its woes but live in reverie!

And it can dwell on moonlight glimmer,
  On evening shade and loneliness ;
And, while the sky grows dim and dimmer,
  Feel no untold and strange distress—

Only a deeper impulse given
  By lonely hour and darkened room,
To solemn thoughts that soar to heaven
  Seeking a life and world to come.

STANZAS.

If thou be in a lonely place,
  If one hour's calm be thine,
As Evening bends her placid face
  O'er this sweet day's decline;
If all the earth and all the heaven
  Now look serene to thee,
As o'er them shuts the summer even,
  One moment—think of me!

Pause, in the lane, returning home;
  'Tis dusk, it will be still:
Pause near the elm, a sacred gloom
  Its breezeless boughs will fill.
Look at that soft and golden light,
  High in the unclouded sky;
Watch the last bird's belated flight,
  As it flits silent by.

Hark! for a sound upon the wind,
A step, a voice, a sigh;
If all be still, then yield thy mind,
Unchecked, to memory.
If thy love were like mine, how blest
That twilight hour would seem,
When, back from the regretted Past,
Returned our early dream!

If thy love were like mine, how wild
Thy longings, even to pain,
For sunset soft, and moonlight mild,
To bring that hour again!
But oft, when in thine arms I lay,
I've seen thy dark eyes shine,
And deeply felt their changeful ray
Spoke other love than mine.

My love is almost anguish now,
It beats so strong and true;
'Twere rapture, could I deem that thou
Such anguish ever knew.

I have been but thy transient flower,
  Thou wert my god divine;
Till checked by death's congealing
    power,
  This heart must throb for thine.

And well my dying hour were blest,
  If life's expiring breath
Should pass, as thy lips gently prest
  My forehead cold in death;
And sound my sleep would be, and
    sweet,
  Beneath the churchyard tree,
If sometimes in thy heart should beat
  One pulse, still true to me.

WATCHING AND WISHING.

OH, would I were the golden light
  That shines around thee now,
As slumber shades the spotless white
  Of that unclouded brow!
It watches through each changeful dream
  Thy features' varied play;
It meets thy waking eyes' soft gleam
  By dawn—by op'ning day.

Oh, would I were the crimson veil
  Above thy couch of snow,
To dye that cheek so soft, so pale,
  With my reflected glow!
Oh, would I were the cord of gold
  Whose tassel set with pearls
Just meets the silken cov'ring's fold
  And rests upon thy curls,

Dishevell'd in thy rosy sleep,
  And shading soft thy dreams;
Across their bright and raven sweep
  The golden tassel gleams!
I would be anything for thee,
  My love—my radiant love—
A flower, a bird, for sympathy,
  A watchful star above.

WHEN THOU SLEEPEST.

WHEN thou sleepest, lulled in night,
  Art thou lost in vacancy?
Does no silent, inward light,
  Softly breaking, fall on thee?
Does no dream on quiet wing
  Float a moment mid that ray,
Touch some answering mental string,
  Wake a note and pass away?

When thou watchest, as the hours
  Mute and blind are speeding on,
O'er that rayless path, where lowers
  Muffled midnight, black and lone;
Comes there nothing hovering near,
  Thought or half reality,
Whispering marvels in thine ear,
  Every word a mystery,

Chanting low an ancient lay,
  Every plaintive note a spell,
Clearing memory's clouds away,
  Showing scenes thy heart loves well?
Songs forgot, in childhood sung,
  Airs in youth beloved and known,
Whispered by that airy tongue,
  Once again are made thine own.

Be it dream in haunted sleep,
  Be it thought in vigil lone,
Drink'st thou not a rapture deep
  From the feeling, 'tis thine own?
All thine own; thou need'st not tell
  What bright form thy slumber blest;—
All thine own; remember well
  Night and shade were round thy rest.

Nothing looked upon thy bed,
  Save the lonely watch-light's gleam;
Not a whisper, not a tread
  Scared thy spirit's glorious dream.

Sometimes, when the midnight gale
Breathed a moan and then was still,
Seemed the spell of thought to fail,
Checked by one ecstatic thrill;

Felt as all external things,
Robed in moonlight, smote thine eye;
Then thy spirit's waiting wings
Quivered, trembled, spread to fly;
Then th' aspirer wildly swelling
Looked, where mid transcendency
Star to star was mutely telling
Heaven's resolve and fate's decree.

Oh! it longed for holier fire
Than this spark in earthly shrine;
Oh! it soared, and higher, higher,
Sought to reach a home divine.
Hopeless quest! soon weak and weary
Flagged the pinion, drooped the plume,
And again in sadness dreary
Came the baffled wanderer home.

And again it turned for soothing
  To th' unfinished, broken dream ;
While, the ruffled current smoothing,
  Thought rolled on her startled stream.
I have felt this cherished feeling,
  Sweet and known to none but me ;
Still I felt it nightly healing
  Each dark day's despondency.

PARTING.

THERE'S no use in weeping,
  Though we are condemned to part:
There's such a thing as keeping
  A remembrance in one's heart:

There's such a thing as dwelling
  On the thought ourselves have nursed,
And with scorn and courage telling
  The world to do its worst.

We'll not let its follies grieve us,
  We'll just take them as they come;
And then every day will leave us
  A merry laugh for home.

When we've left each friend and brother,
  When we're parted wide and far,
We will think of one another,
  As even better than we are.

Every glorious sight above us,
  Every pleasant sight beneath,
We'll connect with those that love us,
  Whom we truly love till death!

In the evening, when we're sitting
  By the fire, perchance alone,
Then shall heart with warm heart meeting,
  Give responsive tone for tone.

We can burst the bonds which chain us,
  Which cold human hands have wrought,
And where none shall dare restrain us
  We can meet again, in thought.

So there's no use in weeping,
  Bear a cheerful spirit still;
Never doubt that Fate is keeping
  Future good for present ill!

APOSTASY.

THIS last denial of my faith,
  Thou, solemn Priest, hast heard;
And, though upon my bed of death,
  I call not back a word.
Point not to thy Madonna, Priest,—
  Thy sightless saint of stone;
She cannot, from this burning breast,
  Wring one repentant moan.

Thou say'st that, when a sinless child,
  I duly bent the knee,
And prayed to what in marble smiled
  Cold, lifeless, mute, on me.
I did. But listen! Children spring
  Full soon to riper youth;
And, for Love's vow and Wedlock's
    ring,
  I sold my early truth.

'Twas not a grey, bare head, like thine,
Bent o'er me, when I said,
"That land and God and Faith are mine,
For which thy fathers bled."
I see thee not, my eyes are dim ;
But well I hear thee say,
" O daughter, cease to think of him
Who led thy soul astray.

"Between you lies both space and time ;
Let leagues and years prevail
To turn thee from the path of crime,
Back to the Church's pale."
And, did I need that thou shouldst tell
What mighty barriers rise
To part me from that dungeon-cell,
Where my loved Walter lies ?

And, did I need that thou shouldst taunt
My dying hour at last,
By bidding this worn spirit pant
No more for what is past ?

Priest—*must* I cease to think of him?
  How hollow rings that word!
Can time, can tears, can distance
      dim
  The memory of my lord?

I said before, I saw not thee,
  Because, an hour agone,
Over my eyeballs, heavily,
  The lids fell down like stone.
But still my spirit's inward sight
  Beholds his image beam
As fixed, as clear, as burning bright,
  As some red planet's gleam.

Talk not of thy Last Sacrament,
  Tell not thy beads for me;
Both rite and prayer are vainly spent,
  As dews upon the sea.
Speak not one word of Heaven above,
  Rave not of Hell's alarms;
Give me but back my Walter's love,
  Restore me to his arms!

Then will the bliss of Heaven be
won;
Then will Hell shrink away,
As I have seen night's terrors shun
The conquering steps of day.
'Tis my religion thus to love,
My creed thus fixed to be;
Not death shall shake, nor Priestcraft
break
My rock-like constancy!

Now go; for at the door there waits
Another stranger guest;
He calls—I come—my pulse scarce
beats,
My heart fails in my breast.
Again that voice—how far away,
How dreary sounds that tone!
And I, methinks, am gone astray
In trackless wastes and lone.

I fain would rest a little while:
Where can I find a stay,
Till dawn upon the hills shall smile,
And show some trodden way?

"I come! I come!" in haste she said;
"'Twas Walter's voice I heard!"
Then up she sprang—but fell back, dead,
His name her latest word.

WINTER STORES.

WE take from life one little share,
And say that this shall be
A space, redeemed from toil and care,
From tears and sadness free.

And, haply, Death unstrings his bow,
And Sorrow stands apart,
And, for a little while, we know
The sunshine of the heart.

Existence seems a summer eve,
Warm, soft, and full of peace ;
Our free, unfettered feelings give
The soul its full release.

A moment, then, it takes the power
  To call up thoughts that throw
Around that charmed and hallowed
    hour,
  This life's divinest glow.

But Time, though viewlessly it flies,
  And slowly, will not stay;
Alike, through clear and clouded skies,
  It cleaves its silent way.

Alike the bitter cup of grief,
  Alike the draught of bliss,
Its progress leaves but moment brief
  For baffled lips to kiss.

The sparkling draught is dried away,
  The hour of rest is gone,
And urgent voices, round us, say,
  "Ho, lingerer, hasten on!"

And has the soul, then, only gained,
  From this brief time of ease,
A moment's rest, when overstrained,
  One hurried glimpse of peace?

No; while the sun shone kindly o'er
us,
And flowers bloomed round our feet,—
While many a bud of joy before us
Unclosed its petals sweet,—

An unseen work within was plying;
Like honey-seeking bee,
From flower to flower, unwearied, fly-
ing,
Laboured one faculty,—

Thoughtful for Winter's future sorrow,
Its gloom and scarcity;
Prescient to-day of want to-morrow,
Toiled quiet Memory.

'Tis she that from each transient pleas-
ure
Extracts a lasting good;
'Tis she that finds, in summer, treasure
To serve for winter's food.

And when Youth's summer day is vanished,
And Age brings winter's stress,
Her stores, with hoarded sweets replenished,
Life's evening hours will bless.

THE MISSIONARY.

PLOUGH, vessel, plough the British main,
Seek the free ocean's wider plain;
Leave English scenes and English skies,
Unbind, dissever English ties;
Bear me to climes remote and strange,
Where altered life, fast-following change,
Hot action, never-ceasing toil,
Shall stir, turn, dig, the spirit's soil;
Fresh roots shall plant, fresh seed shall
sow,
Till a new garden there shall grow,
Cleared of the weeds that fill it now,—
Mere human love, mere selfish yearning,
Which, cherished, would arrest me
yet.
I grasp the plough, there's no returning,
Let me, then, struggle to forget.

But England's shores are yet in view,
And England's skies of tender blue

Arc arches above her guardian sea.
I cannot yet Remembrance flee;
I must again, then, firmly face
That task of anguish to retrace.
Wedded to home—I home forsake;
Fearful of change—I changes make;
Too fond of ease—I plunge in toil;
Lover of calm—I seek turmoil:
Nature and hostile Destiny
  Stir in my heart a conflict wild;
And long and fierce the war will be
  Ere duty both has reconciled.

What other tie yet holds me fast
To the divorced, abandoned past?
Smouldering, on my heart's altar lies
The fire of some great sacrifice,
Not yet half quenched. The sacred steel
But lately struck my carnal will,
My life-long hope, first joy and last,
What I loved well, and clung to fast;
What I wished wildly to retain,
What I renounced with soul-felt pain;

What—when I saw it, axe-struck, perish—
Left me no joy on earth to cherish;
A man bereft—yet sternly now
I do confirm that Jephtha vow:
Shall I retract, or fear, or flee?
Did Christ, when rose the fatal tree
Before him, on Mount Calvary?
'Twas a long fight, hard fought, but won,
And what I did was justly done.

Yet, Helen! from thy love I turned,
When my heart most for thy heart burned;
I dared thy tears, I dared thy scorn—
Easier the death-pang had been borne.
Helen, thou might'st not go with me,
I could not—dared not stay for thee!
I heard, afar, in bonds complain
The savage from beyond the main;
And that wild sound rose o'er the cry
Wrung out by passion's agony;
And even when, with the bitterest tear
I ever shed, mine eyes were dim,
Still, with the spirit's vision clear,
I saw Hell's empire, vast and grim,

Spread on each Indian river's shore,
Each realm of Asia covering o'er.
There, the weak, trampled by the strong,
Live but to suffer—hopeless die;
There pagan-priests, whose creed is Wrong,
Extortion, Lust, and Cruelty,
Crush our lost race—and brimming fill
The bitter cup of human ill;
And I—who have the healing creed,
The faith benign of Mary's Son,
Shall I behold my brother's need,
And, selfishly, to aid him shun?
I—who upon my mother's knees,
In childhood, read Christ's written word,
Received his legacy of peace,
His holy rule of action heard;
I—in whose heart the sacred sense
Of Jesus' love was early felt;
Of his pure, full benevolence,
His pitying tenderness for guilt;
His shepherd-care for wandering sheep,
For all weak, sorrowing, trembling things,

His mercy vast, his passion deep
  Of anguish for man's sufferings;
I—schooled from childhood in such lore—
  Dared I draw back or hesitate,
When called to heal the sickness sore
  Of those far-off and desolate?
Dark, in the realm and shades of Death,
  Nations, and tribes, and empires lie,
But even to them the light of Faith
  Is breaking on their sombre sky:
And be it mine to bid them raise
  Their drooped heads to the kindling scene,
And know and hail the sunrise blaze
  Which heralds Christ the Nazarene.
I know how Hell the veil will spread
  Over their brows and filmy eyes,
And earthward crush the lifted head
  That would look up and seek the skies;
I know what war the fiend will wage
  Against that soldier of the Cross,
Who comes to dare his demon rage,
  And work his kingdom shame and loss.

Yes, hard and terrible the toil
Of him who steps on foreign soil,
Resolved to plant the gospel vine,
Where tyrants rule and slaves repine;
Eager to lift Religion's light
Where thickest shades of mental night
Screen the false god and fiendish rite;
Reckless that missionary blood,
Shed in wild wilderness and wood,
Has left, upon the unblest air,
The man's deep moan—the martyr's prayer.
I know my lot—I only ask
Power to fulfil the glorious task;
Willing the spirit, may the flesh
Strength for the day receive afresh.
May burning sun or deadly wind
Prevail not o'er an earnest mind;
May torments strange or direst death
Nor trample truth, nor baffle faith.
Though such blood-drops should fall from me
As fell in old Gethsemane,

Welcome the anguish, so it gave
More strength to work—more skill to
    save.
And, oh! if brief must be my time,
If hostile hand or fatal clime
Cut short my course—still o'er my grave,
Lord, may thy harvest whitening wave.
So I the culture may begin,
Let others thrust the sickle in;
If but the seed will faster grow,
May my blood water what I sow!

What! have I ever trembling stood,
And feared to give to God that blood?
What! has the coward love of life
Made me shrink from the righteous
    strife?
Have human passions, human fears
Severed me from those Pioneers
Whose task is to march first, and trace
Paths for the progress of our race?
It has been so; but grant me, Lord,
Now to stand steadfast by Thy word!
Protected by salvation's helm,
  Shielded by faith, with truth begirt,

To smile when trials seek to whelm
  And stand mid testing fires unhurt!
Hurling Hell's strongest bulwarks down,
  Even when the last pang thrills my breast,
When death bestows the martyr's crown,
  And calls me into Jesus' rest.
Then for my ultimate reward—
Then for the world-rejoicing word—
The voice from Father—Spirit—Son:
"Servant of God, well hast thou done!"

Lightning Source UK Ltd.
Milton Keynes UK

177032UK00001B/133/P

9 781446 009758